Tell It Like It Is,
Make No Bones About It

BOOK 2

CAROL S. STEPHENS

authorHOUSE®

AuthorHouse™
1663 Liberty Drive
Bloomington, IN 47403
www.authorhouse.com
Phone: 1 (800) 839-8640

Published by AuthorHouse 09/25/2015

ISBN: 978-1-5049-5065-7 (sc)
ISBN: 978-1-5049-5064-0 (e)

Print information available on the last page.

Any people depicted in stock imagery provided by Thinkstock are models, and such images are being used for illustrative purposes only.
Certain stock imagery © Thinkstock.

This book is printed on acid-free paper.

Because of the dynamic nature of the Internet, any web addresses or links contained in this book may have changed since publication and may no longer be valid. The views expressed in this work are solely those of the author and do not necessarily reflect the views of the publisher, and the publisher hereby disclaims any responsibility for them.

KJV
Scripture quotations marked KJV are from the Holy Bible, King James Version (Authorized Version). First published in 1611.
Quoted from the KJV Classic Reference Bible. Copyright © 1983 by The Zondervan Corporation.

TABLE OF CONTENTS

LOVE AND GRATITUDE

So thankful to God for giving me the gift of writing and painting, the two things I love to do and blessing me with a good husband precious children and grandchildren.

LORD, I DON'T UNDERSTAND

LORD, I don't understand how You always were and always
Will be-
I don't understand the trinity; Father, Son and Holy Spirit-
I don't understand how You created the heavens and the earth,
Light and darkness, sun,-
Moon and stars- The magnificent oceans and majestic mountains-
I don't understand the miraculous, intricate way we are made
And able to produce-
Precious children; some brilliant, some average-like me-
LORD, I don't understand Your virgin birth and why You left
Your beautiful, peaceful, sinless-
Throne in heaven to come walk with a sinful, corrupted, selfish
People-
I don't understand why You willingly suffered a cruel and
Agonizing death upon a crude-
Rugged cross when You were sinless-
I don't understand eternity or how You could possibly still
Continue to love us-

Unconditionally and forgive us when we are so undeserving-
LORD, I don't understand why prophets of old and saints down
Through the ages, willingly-
Gave up everything to follow You, even unto death-
I don't understand why You have let Satan have his rule over
Earth and our sinful nature-
Or unbelief in so great a salvation-
I don't understand hate, wars, killings and vicious crimes on our
Innocent, children, young-
People and adults-
I don't understand the presence of Your angels all around and
Your Holy Spirit indwelling us-
LORD, I don't understand all Your precious Word, Your mighty
Ways, Your righteousness, and
Most of all, Your grace-
I don't understand LORD, but.......I BELIEVE!

LORD, CHANGE MY HEART

Lord, there are still places in
My heart that I have not
Turned over to You-
I can't do it alone even though
You know I've tried to-
There is still a barrier that I've
Built up over many years-
That wall has been put there by
Scars and many tears-
I pray that You will break-
That barrier down----

That You will change my heart-
And bring me around-
To being more-
Caring, loving, giving-
And Lord, most of all,-
More forgiving-
I want to be what You would-
Choose me to be-
I want to be more like You-
And less like me--

JESUS SAYS/SATAN SAYS

Jesus says-"Come ye who are heavy laden and I will give you rest-"
Satan says-"Who needs rest, I'll just dull your problems with Booze and drugs-"
Jesus says-"I am the same yesterday, today and forever-"
Satan says-"The Bible is outdated- God doesn't mean all those old Rules-"
Jesus says-"All have sinned and come short of the glory of God-"
Satan says-"What is sin?-Do what is right in your own eyes-"
Jesus says-"Fear God and keep My commandments-"
Satan says-"Wow, just because He has written a Book, He thinks He is God-"
Jesus says-"Set your mind on things above, not on things of the earth-"
Satan says-"That's malarky!-How are you supposed to take care Of things-
　　　On earth with your mind elsewhere?-
Jesus says-"Enter by the narrow gate, because narrow is the Gate and-
　　　Difficult is the way which leads to life, few find it-"
Satan says-'My way is broad and easy to find-Why make it difficult?"-

Jesus says-"I will come on a white horse, in a white robe to judge And make war-"
Satan says-"I guess I'm the bad guy on the black horse, with a Black robe and hat-"
　　　"At least I won't judge you-"
Jesus says-"No more sun and no more moon-I will be your light-"
Satan says-"We will have a nice little campfire-That will be our light-"
Jesus says-"No more tears, no more dying- forever with God-"
Satan says-"We'll have plenty of weeping and gnashing of teeth, You'll be-
　　　With me forever-"
Jesus says- With arms open wide, "I LOVE YOU-"
Satan says-With a wicked grin," GOTCHA!"

****

As for God, His way is perfect, the Word of the Lord is proven. He is a shield to all who trust Him.

Psalm 18:30

5

GOD IS THE WAY

Jesus, Your life You gave-
For our life to save-
In Adam and Eve it did begin-
Our lives of work, struggles and sin-
A perfect, peaceful garden was their place-
But they listened to Satan and sin was a disgrace-
Come what may-
"Whatever," you say-
If from your evil ways you do not turn-
At the end of life you will surely burn-
Do you not know the way?-
Here's what the Lord does say-

From your sins and evil ways repent-
And on his way, Satan you have sent-
Believe in Jesus Christ the Lord-
For He alone is the living Word-

****

Jesus said to him, "I am the way, the truth,
And the life. No one comes to the Father
Except through Me."

John 14:6

PICTURE THIS

You are in a long line that must stretch for miles-
Every one is solemn, no one cracking jokes-
There are no small children in the line-

At the front of the line is someone who can read your heart-
Two huge signs capture your attention-
One is on the right and the other on the left-
The one on the right says, "Those with a loving, forgiving heart-"
The one on the left says, "Those with a greedy, self-serving heart-"

You can see a larger crowd of people going to the left-
They are weeping-
You start to sweat-
Your life flashes before you-

You pat yourself on the back remembering the times that you-
Gave to the poor, the church, the missionaries and the hungry-
But----Was this a tax write-off?-
You went to church regularly, but was this out of habit or duty-
Was this to hear God's Word or about what others might think-
Of you if you didn't go?-

Then you think, there are people that you just can't feel sorry for-
They don't even try to help themselves-
They just want a handout-
And of course you can't love murderers, child molesters, thieves-
And just plain bad people-

And so maybe I stole a few small things and told a few white lies-
So what! I've got money but I earned it-
I'm a lot better than most people-
I've stored up for my retirement. It's my life-

DETOUR

While barreling down the road without a care in the world-
Maybe listening to your favorite music-
And all of a sudden you come upon a sign that says, "DETOUR."-

To me detours are a very scary, unknown and unfamiliar territory-
There could be many reasons for a detour-
Bridge out, road wash out, construction or even a huge wreck-
We have to slow down and give it our strict attention-

I think about children growing up in church-
They are so happy learning about Jesus and His love-

Then when they are teens and graduating from high school-
They decide to take a detour from God's Word- How scary!-
I guess you can say its rebellion but against who I don't know-
Maybe God, maybe parents or maybe society-

They decide to dabble in drugs, alcohol and sex-
They get in with the wrong crowd-
They stop thinking about God and the consequences-
How much they are hurting family, others and themselves-

This detour is dangerous and very risky-
This detour can change the rest of their lives-
Some don't even live through this detour-
Some might come out maimed for life
A few might make it back to God-
To live their lives for Him- back on the right track-
Thankful to have survived the detour-
Praise God for those who make it out alive-

Even grown people can take detours away from God-
Detours for them can also be a scary- unfamiliar territory-
And up ahead - the unknown-
They might decide to dabble in drugs, alcohol and sex-
They might also get in with the wrong crowd-
And stop thinking about the consequences-
How much they are hurting family, others and themselves-

LORD, TAKE AWAY MY ITCH

When you have an itch, does it help to keep scratching it?
Does it make it go away?
Oh it feels good for a while---but then it gets worse-
Sometimes it bleeds-
It will never go away until we quit scratching it-
Until we put medicine on it to heal it-
I think of Satan and sin this way-
When we sin, it feels good for a while---But-
It festers and becomes a bad sore-
It will not go away unless we seek God's help-
Only Jesus can forgive our sins and take away our itch-
Only Jesus can save our souls-

We need to recognize that we have sin in our lives-
We need to seek God and His forgiveness-
We need to ask Jesus to come into our hearts to change us-
We need to pray each day for God's strength-
We need to ask God for His will for our lives-
We need to be on our knees thanking and praising God-

****

If we say that we have no sin, we deceive ourselves, and
The truth is not in us. If we confess our sins, He is faithful
And just to forgive us our sins and to cleanse us from all
Unrighteousness.

1 John 1:8,9

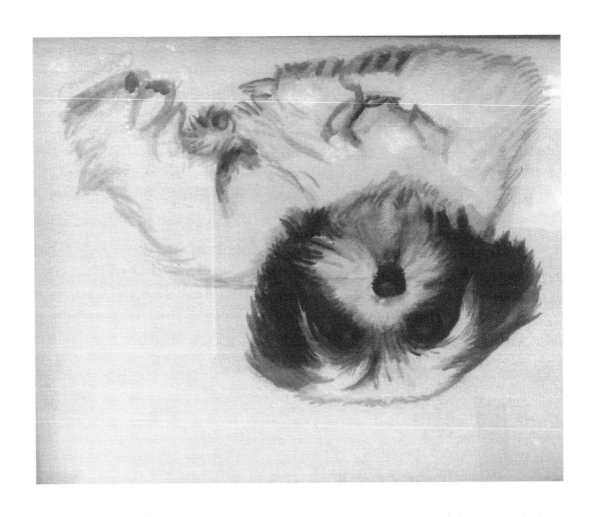

LORD, YOU ARE NOT JUST A CASUAL ACQUAINTANCE

Lord, so many people are so casual about You-
They treat You like You're just another everyday decision-
They treat You with the same casualness as they would in-
Deciding what to wear that day or where they should eat-
Some might even treat You as if You are no more than a stranger-
They meet in a grocery store- A pleasant smile and acknowledgement-
Lord, their main focus is on themselves and what is going on around them-
Some are so caught up in their own lives they forget about You-

Lord, You are our Creator, King of Kings and Lord of Lords-
You deserve more than a casual thanks at mealtime-
You deserve our undying love and devotion-
Jesus died for you and me and all our sins-

****

All we like sheep have gone astray; we have turned everyone-
To his own way, and the Lord hath laid on Him the iniquity-
Of us all.

Isaiah 53:6

BRING ON THE FLOWERS

God sends flowers because He cares-
God sends flowers when you're in despair-
He sends flowers to soothe our hurt-
When it seems nothing else will work-

All the time, flowers are inviting-
Mostly unexpected and so exciting-
So many colors and such a display-
"I love you," they seem to say-

Oh what a beautiful, amazing sight-
To see a field of flowers so awesome and bright-
If your troubles seem an overflowing bowl-
God will send flowers to lift your soul-

After a quenching rain, God sends flowers that are wild-
He seems to say, "All is forgiven, you're My child"-
Springtime seems to be new beginnings-
With an abundance of flowers with no ending-

As welcoming as flowers are to our eyes-
God adds even more with colorful, elegant butterflies-
And how about the bashful smile on a child's face-
As he hands you a tiny flower, delicate as lace-

A bridal bouquet and lots of flowers are the setting-
For a handsome groom and gorgeous bride's wedding-
Flowers for a weary mother of a precious baby she tenderly caresses-
Knowing God is the One who truly and faithfully blesses-

When our days are gloomy and gray-
Flowers are like the sun's golden ray-
Our spirits flowers will lift-
So delightful, what a gift-

With flowers we show our love and respect at the grave side-
Hoping that they knew Jesus, and in heaven abide-
Jesus sees our tears and sorrows-
And with flowers says do not fear tomorrows-

Flowers, looking to the sun, their heads gently nod-
Giving praise to their Creator, Almighty God-
Who lovingly smells their sweet fragrance-

And delights in watching them sway and dance-

Our God is loving and compassionate-
Giving us the gift of flowers to appreciate-
So when the vision of flowers make you feel alive-
Praise God with an enthusiastic "High Five!"-

****

Consider the lilies, how they grow:
They neither toil nor spin;
And yet I say to you, even Solomon in all his glory
Was not arrayed like one of these.

Luke 12:27

GOD'S SUN/GOD'S SON

I have plants in the house that I have to keep turning around-
Because they keep turning towards the sun-
When I turn them around so the other side is toward the light-
Source, it causes a more even growth-
If I don't keep turning them, they grow lopsided-
Aren't we drawn to the warmth of the sun on a chilly morning?
After dreary damp days, don't we just want to go outside-
And soak up the sun-
We love to see children playing on the beach, lake or even a-
Playground in the wonderful sunshine-
The benefits of the sun and exercise are good for us-
Like plants and trees are drawn toward the sun-
We should be drawn toward God's Son, Jesus Christ-
To His nurturing love and warmth-

Are you turning towards God's Son?-
Growing out of darkness and into the light-
Or are you lopsided because you are staying in one place, sin-
Do you soak up His Word-receiving His benefits?-
We have to be cautious-by not believing and getting burned-
Only dwell on the truth of God-don't get side-tracked-

****

Blessed be the name of the Lord from this time forth and for
Evermore. From the rising of the sun unto the going down of
The same, the Lord's name is to be praised.

Psalm 113:2,3

LORD, YOU ARE REAL

Do you knock on wood for good luck?-
Do you throw money in a fountain and make a wish?-
A penny found heads up is good luck but tails up is bad.-
What about walking under a ladder being bad luck-
Is a black cat crossing your path really bad luck?-

How many crazy ideas like these have we grown up with?-
These are handed down from generation to generation
I heard these and many, many more--
My grandchildren have the sweetest black cat that's not bad luck-
Do you really think your luck hinges on any of these?

Putting our faith in God is not superstition or something unstable-
When we pray to God it has nothing to do with luck-
When we trust in God it is faith, not making a wish-
Our belief in Jesus Christ is truth, not fiction-

God is our creator—He knows us and we need to know Him-

Have you put your trust in a God who knows your every thought?-
A God who gave His only Son to die for our sins—Jesus was sinless-
A son who died on that cruel cross but rose the third day-
Jesus is now at the right hand of God in heaven praying for you-
A God who loves you more than your mind can understand-

****

For the time will come when they will not endure sound doctrine,
But according to their own desires, because they have itching ears,
They will heap up for themselves teachers, and they will turn their
Ears away from the truth, and be turned aside to fables.

2 timothy 4:3,4

27

SHELBY

BROCK

AUSTIN

JACKSON

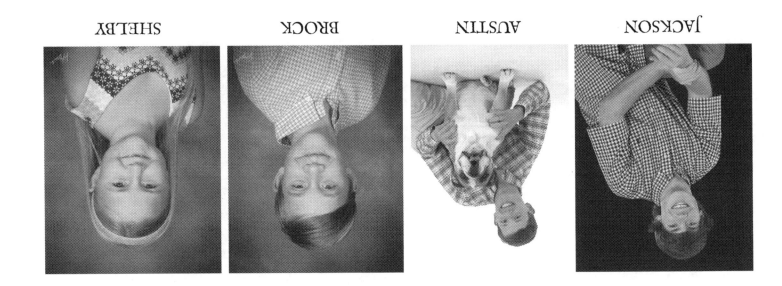

GOD HAS A FUNNY BONE?

I think God truly enjoyed creating the animals-
Just look around-

Hippopotamus-Huge with short stubby legs-
Monkey-A long tail to hang by-
Fire-fly-His backend lights up-
Turtle and Armadillo-Their house is on their back
Gnats-Are so bothersome-

Manatee-So big and gentle-
Snake-Slithers on the ground-
Raccoon-Has two black eyes-
Giraffe-Has a really long neck and legs-
Eagle-Majestic and king of the mountain-

Cow-Only has lower teeth-
Porcupine-Covered in sharp needles
Skunk-Can spray a really foul smell-
Elephant-Huge ears and a long trunk-
Camel-One or two big humps on his back-

Horse-beautiful and fun to ride-
Lions and Tigers-So powerful-
Ant-Tiny, but a hard worker-
Peacock-Gorgeous tail that fans out-
Anteater-Long snout and sticky tongue

Kangaroo-Powerful back legs and a front pouch-
Zebra-So many stripes-
Bear-Big and dangerous-
Alligator-Very deadly with leather-like hide
Puppies and kittens-So loveable-

So many more animals, fish and birds that we don't
Even know about, and God created each one of them
And knows where they are-

****

For every beast of the forest is Mine and the cattle on a
Thousand hills. I know all the birds of the mountains, and
The wild beasts of the field are Mine.

Psalm 50:10,11

29

A STORM IS COMING-A STORM IS COMING

BREAKING NEWS! ALERT! BE PREPARED-
Baton down the hatches- cover the windows-
Most of us know how to prepare for a storm-
Have lots of drinking water, flash light batteries-
candles, matches, and a weather radio-
You need food that doesn't need cooking or refrigeration-
Find a safe place away from windows—
The list goes on and on, but most important-
Be prepared!

JESUS IS COMING-JESUS IS COMING

BREAKING NEWS! ALERT! BE PREPARED-
Baton down the hatches-Get ready-
Most of us know how to prepare for a storm-
But are we prepared for the second coming of Jesus?-
We don't have to prepare ourselves physically-
But we have to be prepared spiritually-

Our hearts need to be right with God-
His Word living in our hearts and minds-
His praise on our lips-
Thanksgiving in our hearts-
Helping others and praying for all-
Living each day as if He is coming today-

We should be prepared at all times-
We won't have a news cast that tells us -
Exactly when Jesus is coming again-
We won't have weather balloons to warn us-
No physic or prophet can tell us-
Not even the angels in heaven know-

Why would we be warned ahead of time of Jesus' coming?
So sinners could keep on sinning until the day before-
And than repent?-No!
If we knew the exact time a thief would break into our home-
We would be prepared-

God wants us to be prepared for Jesus' coming-
We should watch and pray daily-
In God's Word are signs of His coming-
We are not to fear but be prepared-

God says "For as the lightening cometh out of the east-
Shineth even unto the west; so shall the coming of the-
Son of Man be-

++++

But of that day and that hour knoweth no man,
No not the angels which are in heaven,
Neither the Son, but the Father.

Mark 13:32

A BATTLE

Can you imagine going into battle and God telling you to choose your men-
By the way they drink water from a river?-
We're talking about 10,000 men.-
Can you imagine running along to see if the men drank the water by lapping-
It up straight from the river like a dog laps it or gets down on their knees to-
Drink that way-

Of course, since God asked Gideon to do it this way, God helped.
Gideon was to choose only 300 men to take into battle with him against-
The Midianites-
God wanted the number of men to be reduced so He would get the glory-
And Israel could not take the credit for winning-

The Bible is not dull- There are so many stories in it that we should learn from-
There are stories of healing, battles, miracles, prophecy and a strong faith of-
The men and women of old-
Also it tells us of what happens when you don't believe and don't obey God-

God is our creator-He knew us before we were born-In fact, He knew us-
Before He created the heavens and earth-He knows our name, our hearts, our
Thoughts and the precise moment we are going to die-He already knows if we-
Are going to believe in Jesus Christ as our Lord and Savior-He is King of Kings-
And Lord of Lords-All authority has been given to Him-

Do you truly believe in your heart and not just a head knowledge?-Be positive-
That you know the answer to this crucial question-Has Jesus prepared a place
For you in heaven?-Our life is but a tiny speck in comparing it to eternity-
Eternity is the absence of time- There is no end-

****

I am the Lord, that is My name; and My glory I will not give to another,
Nor My praise to carved images.

Isaiah 42:8

IS YOUR DOOR LOCKED?

We all need to keep our doors locked for our safety-
And the safety of our children and grandchildren-
Our home doors and the doors of our cars should stay locked-
There will always be thieves who would rather steal than work-
To kill for drugs or what little money you might have-
There will always be sick, unstable people lurking about-
That want to harm our children-
We have to do what we can to keep safe-

Have you ever thought of your heart as a door?-
Satan will break into the door of your heart like a thief-
Is the door of your heart tightly locked and bolted-
Against The Word of God?-
Your heart is the center of your being-
Your heart is the door to your soul-
What you feel in your heart is who you are-

If your heart is wicked and full of sin, that's who you are-
If your heart is compassionate and full of love, that's who
you are-

Jesus knows your very heart and soul-
He wants you to open the door to your heart-
And in return He will be the door for you to enter-
And be saved-

No one can ever rob you of God's salvation-
It's yours for eternity-

****

I am the door. If anyone enters by Me, he will be saved,
And will go in and out and find pasture.
The thief does not come except to steal, and to kill,
And to destroy.
I have come that they may have life and that they
May have it more abundantly.

John 10:9, 10

FIGHT AGAINST GOD?

Would you dare think of such a thing-
But isn't that what we are doing when we don't believe?-
Isn't that what we are doing by not obeying His commandments?-
Do you know what going against God is like?-

Are you prepared to go against someone who spoke:-
The universe into existence-
Created man and woman-
Made the sun stand still for almost a whole day for Joshua-

Can call upon legions of His angels-
Parted the Red Sea for His people, the Israelites to pass through-
Then caused it to close over Pharaoh's army-
Can cause the stars to fall to earth-

Make thunder roll and lightening flash and strike-
Make a donkey talk to Balaam-
Make King Nebuchadnezzar eat grass like an oxen for seven years-
Until the King praised God-

Caused famines, rivers to dry up, and crops to burn up-
Can send rain or withhold it-
Just by His look, make the earth tremble and the mountains shake-
Knows exactly when a sparrow falls to the ground-

Made Lazarus, who was dead for four days, rise again-
Made a huge wall crumble around Jericho after men with-
Trumpets marched around it seven times, obeying God-
Turned a rod into a snake and back to a rod again for Moses-

Caused a big fish to swallow Jonah and then vomit him up-
On dry land after three days and three nights, still alive-
Cured a man from leprosy by his washing seven times –
In the Jordon River-----Naaman obeyed God-

Rained fire and brimstone down on Sodom and Gomorrah-
Turned Lot's wife into a pillar of salt because she disobeyed God-
Fed over five thousand with five barley loaves and two small fish-
And filled twelve baskets with the leftovers-

BODY AND SOUL

We try to take care of our bodies-
We exercise, some a little-
Some very religiously-
We go to the doctor-
We go to the dentist-

We take vitamins and other healthy supplements-
We bathe, wash our hair, brush teeth, and clip nails-
We put on sunscreen, sunglasses and hats-
We put on perfume and good smelling lotions-

All this and more we do in the name of good health-
And to live longer-
But------------------------

Are you taking care of your soul?-
Have you accepted Jesus Christ-
As your Lord and Savior?-

Have you confessed your sins-

And turned your life around?-
Have you given your life to God?
Have you let Him cleanse-
Your heart and soul?-

Have you let Jesus Christ-
Save your soul from-
An eternity in Hell-
To an eternity with Him-
In heaven?-

Believe on Jesus Christ and-
Let Him save your soul today-

****

Seek the Lord while He may be found,
Call upon Him while He is near.

Isaiah 55:6

A TASTE OF HELL

I work at being healthy- Even joined a gym-
I read a lot about what I should eat-
And what medicines I should not have to take-
I wanted to lower my cholesterol without a statin drug-

A friend told me her husband lowered his with Niacin-
She might have even told me what dosage to start with-
But, as usual I jump in with both feet, not testing the water-
I went to the health food store and bought a small bottle of Niacin-

My husband was home so I decided to take one after lunch-
The bottle said you might get a flush but I figured it would –
Not last more than a few minutes-
Boy was I wrong!-

After five minutes, I started itching all over-
My heart started beating real fast-
When I could stand it no longer, I ran for the shower-
As I ran past the bathroom mirror, I looked and was beet red-

Cool water didn't help and neither did cold water-
I felt like I was going to pass out-
I grabbed a towel and barely made it to my bed-
My husband thought I was dying-

We had the fan going and he brought cold cream-
I had a slow burn from my head to my toes-
Nothing helped and it lasted for an hour and a half-
I thought about those poor souls in hell forever and ever-

Hell is a place of utter darkness and torment-
A place of loneliness and suffering-
Complete isolation with no hope and no escape-
God doesn't want to send you there-

****

For the wages of sin is death, but the gift of God is
Eternal life in Christ Jesus our Lord.

Romans 6:23

AUTOMATIC

How many times have we done something so many times,-
That it just becomes automatic-
Have you ever gotten down the road and couldn't remember-
Locking the door to your home?-
Have you arrived somewhere and couldn't remember the drive?-
How about driving right past your destination-
Because your mind is on something else?-
It's really scary-

What about cruise control-
All you have to do is steer-Your mind can wander-
When asked how you are-
Do we automatically say "fine"-
How much of your life is automatic-

Do you automatically go to church and when you leave,-
Can't remember what was said-
We should never be on auto-pilot with God-
We should be alert, listening to every word-
Knowingly praising God and worshipping Him-

Changing our routine will make us more alert-
On automatic we are no better off than a robot-
No feelings, no life, no excitement- just existing-
How boring!-
God gave us a wonderful, unique mind-
Wake up to God's blessings each day-

****

"Thus says the Lord of hosts, consider your ways."

Haggai 1:7

ARE YOU WICKED?

Do you enjoy hurting people?-
Spreading vicious gossip about them-
Putting people down so you look better-
Bullying those that seem to be weak-
Always criticizing everyone and everything?-

Are you troubled and restless?-
Never happy or content with life as it is-
Always after things that make you feel better-
Climbing the ladder of success to feel more important-
Neglecting those you have stepped on or over?-

Are you always jealous and envious of others?-
Taunting those with a strong faith in God-
Seeing evil as good and good as evil-

Never respecting those with authority over you-
Never giving of yourself or your money?-

Does hate and restlessness fill your heart and soul?-
Do lies and profanity come from your mouth daily?-
Does your mind dwell on evil?-
Have you ever known love?-
Do you truly want to change?-

****

But the wicked are like the troubled sea. When it
Cannot rest, whose waters cast up mire and dirt.
There is no peace, saith my God, to the wicked.

Isaiah 58:20, 21

IF ONLY WE COULD CHANGE THE PAST

But we can't change the past-
So why make it last-
If on the past you have dwelt too long-
Bringing up the same old story and song-
Everyone else we have to blame-
When it's really us, that's a shame-

From your past take what you learn-
And from your anger and bitterness turn-
The past is over and done-
Gone forever, so from it run-

All the past problems that had you reeling-
Forgive yourself first, then others and start healing-
As dawn breaks on a new day-
Strength from God will come as you pray-

To forgive us our sins is why Jesus came-
So we need to forgive others in Jesus' name-

****

Let your speech always be with grace,
Seasoned with salt that you may know
How you ought to answer each one-

Colossians 4:6

HEAVEN BOUND

You can't get to heaven on a technicality-
So let's just face this reality-
This is where we will begin-
Christ the Lord died for our sin-
Turn from your ugly ways and repent-
Or to an eternity in hell you will be sent-

This world can only offer sorrows-
With not much hope for better tomorrows-
Oh, temporary happiness we might see-
But nothing compares with what heaven will be-

We're all on a path of destruction-
So on our hearts let God begin construction-
And if life in heaven is your destination-
To God will be your ultimate dedication-
He will surely wipe clean your slate-
And tomorrow's troubles will surely wait-

So take a break from your daily grind-
Relax, thank God and unwind-
He loves you and is always near-
And your prayers, He will always hear-

****

For You, Lord, are good, and ready to forgive,
And abundant in mercy to all those who-
Call upon You.

Psalm 86:5

LORD, I WORRY THAT I WORRY

As a child of God's, I know that I should not worry-
I should completely trust in God-
And not be concerned with daily problems-
So I worry that I worry-

I know it's wrong to fret and fume-
To try to work things out on my own-
Many nights with no sleep, tossing and turning-
So I worry that I worry-

When I look back over the years-
I see God's hand in my life leading me-
I see unnecessary fears and anxieties-
So I worry that I worry-

God has truly and abundantly blessed me-
He has given me a good life-
He is still with me and watching over me-
So I worry that I worry-

****

Therefore do not worry about tomorrow,
For tomorrow will worry about its own things.
Sufficient for the day is its own trouble.

Matthew 6:34

LORD, ARE WE FOOLING OURSELVES?

In our minds, we believe-
In our minds we know of Jesus-
In our minds we know God created the heavens and the earth-
In our minds we know God created man
In our minds we know God created all living creatures-

In our minds we know God gives us life-
In our minds we know there is a heaven and a hell-
In our minds we know between right and wrong-
In our minds we know we can ask forgiveness from God-
In our minds we trust God, but maybe not completely-

In our minds we think we are too good for God to send us to hell-
In our minds we are better than others-
In our minds we are looking for praise and recognition-
In our minds we are doing what is right in our eyes, not God's-
In our minds we really don't think God is paying attention to us-

But----God is all knowing and all seeing-
God looks at our hearts-

Do we know God's holy Word-
Do we talk to God daily-
Do we love and forgive others-
Do we pray for others-
Do we help the poor, needy and sick

Do we thank God for everything-
Do we acknowledge God for who He is-
Do we seek God with all our heart, soul and mind-
Do we know God, the Father, Jesus, the Son and the Holy Spirit-
Do we truly bow down and worship them-

++++

Lord, who shall abide in thy tabernacle?
Who shall dwell in thy holy hill?
He that walketh uprightly, and worketh righteousness,
And speaketh the truth in his heart.

Psalm 15: 1, 2

59

LORD, I PRAY FOR THE LOST

Do you feel my prayers?-
Do you feel the agony in my heart for you?
Do you feel the desperation I have for your soul?-
The desperation for you to know and believe in God-

Not just knowing there is a God somewhere-
A higher power somewhere out there-
A god made by human hands-
A god that cannot hear, see or answer prayers-

Not just a person who thinks he is a god-
Someone whom Satan sends to deceive you-
A person of witchcraft or sorcery-
A god who wants you to do evil things-

But the One true living God-
The God who created the universe-
The God who created man and woman-
The God who holds the oceans, moon, sun and stars in place-

The only God who can save your soul-
The God who created hell for Satan and his fallen angels-
The God who created heaven for all true believers-
The only true living God who can cleanse your sins-

A God of love and mercy-
A gracious, compassionate God-
A God who has a plan for your life-
A God you can trust to be faithful-

****

But He, because He continues forever, has an unchangeable-
Priesthood, therefore He is also able to save to the uttermost-
Those who come to God through Him, since He always lives-
To make intercession for them.

Hebrews 7:24,25

JESUS OFFERS AN OLIVE BRANCH

I'm at your door-
I'll knock once more-
Maybe 2,3 or even four-
Maybe no more-

Don't turn Me away-
Salvation is here today-
It is here to stay-
I'll take your burdens away-

I'm holding out an Olive branch-
Grab hold while you have the chance-
For Me to take away your strife-
And give you peace and eternal life-

Open the door to your heart wide-
And let the love of Jesus settle inside-
And His Words in you abide-
And His Holy Spirit always reside-

Jesus Christ never changes-
Everything is as He arranges-
Some day we will see His wonderful face-
But only through God's love and grace-

****

Fear not, for I am with you;
Be not dismayed, for I am
Your God, I will strengthen you,
Yes, I will help you, I will uphold
You with My righteous right hand.

Isaiah 41:10

WHO DO YOU SAY THAT I AM?

Jesus asked this of His disciples-
He will ask this of each one of us-
Not who our husband or wife or brother or sister
Or even friends say He is-

But each of us alone-

It is a question every single person in the whole-
World will have to answer to Jesus-

How will you answer?-

****

Simon Peter answered and said,
"You are the Christ, the Son of the living
God."

Mathew 16:16

Printed in the United States
By Bookmasters